BULLETIN BOARD DESIGNS FOR THE CHRISTIAN CLASSROOM

by Carolyn Berg

Concordia

Publishing House
St. Louis

Copyright © 1984 Concordia Publishing House
3558 S. Jefferson Avenue, St. Louis, MO 63118-3968
Manufactured in the United States of America

Library of Congress Cataloging in Publication Data

Berg, Carolyn, 1943-
   Bulletin board designs for the Christian classroom.

1. Christian education—Bulletin boards.   I. Title.
BV1535.25.B47   1984   268'.635   84-7044
ISBN 0-570-03930-4

1 2 3 4 5 6 7 8 9 10 MAL 93 92 91 90 89 88 87 86 85 84

Contents

Christian Bulletin Boards

Bulletin Board Ideas for September—June

Christian Bulletin Boards

What Is the Purpose?

Is there such a thing as a "bulletin board" ministry? Most definitely. Just as God gives each of us our special talents, He also gives us avenues to express them for His glory. A message on a bulletin board may be a ray of hope to one in despair; it may be a signpost to lead a searching soul toward Christ; it may give the believer a deeper appreciation of God's love; it may give the unbeliever something to think about—maybe just enough to let the Holy Spirit begin His work.

As long as our messages are Christ-centered and based upon God's Holy Word we can be sure they are effective: "So shall My word be that goeth forth out of My mouth: it shall not return unto Me void, but it shall accomplish that which I please, and it shall prosper in the thing whereto I sent it" (Is. 55:11).

Where to Start?

When confronted with the task of preparing a bulletin board on a given topic, there is only one place to start: "Take it to the Lord in prayer!" No task is ever too small or too large to ask for God's help.

Soon you will find the Lord leading you to certain passages of Scripture, singing a meaningful line of a hymn, or giving you a visual picture of a sermon. He will always find a way to show you what He wants to say and how He wants to say it.

Materials to Use
Background

The materials selected for the background should be appropriate for the theme of the bulletin board. For example, a bright red glossy paper would be suitable for a joyous festival such as Christmas; the humility of burlap would be more appropriate for the Lenten season.

Of all the materials that can be used successfully as bulletin board backgrounds, paper is probably the most common and most versatile. Bulletin board paper in solid colors on large rolls is available from most school supply companies. If your funds are limited and if you will need only a few bulletin board changes during the year, it is wise to begin with a single roll of white paper. As your needs expand, your selections will most likely be red, blue, and green. These colors can provide the necessary background throughout an entire church/school year.

Construction paper (preferably 12" x 18") can also be used as a background. This works best on smaller areas (less than 30" x 40"). When construction paper is used to cover large surfaces, the effect can be a bit "patchy." Construction paper backgrounds are most effective when many things will be mounted, thus covering most of the seams.

Gift-wrapping paper also makes an interesting background, but it must be chosen with care. When gift wrap is used to cover an entire board, select a design with a tiny pattern. The background should not be so busy or so loud that it overpowers the message to be displayed. Foil gift wrap may be also used as a background. If a background is done in foil, the letters, borders, symbols, etc., should be limited to one color. White looks best on a background of red or green foil, while black looks best on silver or gold foil. Remember too that the kind of lighting available in relation to the position of the bulletin board can create a glare on a foil background. Be sure to take this into consideration when deciding upon foil backgrounds.

Wallpaper also provides an excellent background. Exercise care here too, so that the background will not overpower the message. Subtle stripes and single-colored textures are best suited to add interest without detracting from the message. Sometimes prints will work out, *if* they are appropriate for the theme of the message. When considering a print, it is best to choose from only those things found in God's creation: trees, foliage, flowers, rocks, wood grain, etc. It is best to avoid animal prints and prints with large brightly-colored flowers. Use only small prints with subtle coloring. Monochromatic color schemes (several shades and intensities of one basic color) provide the most attractive backgrounds.

Often lumber companies, paint stores, hardware stores, or department stores run promotional sales on roll ends or discontinued patterns. Sometimes these stores will give away the unsold ends when their sales are finished. (Many stores seem willing to donate such items for school or church purposes, since it makes for good public relations.)

Carpet can also be used effectively as a bulletin board background. Solid colors work out better than prints, plaids, etc. Short-napped flat surfaces are preferable to shag or sculptured textures. Jute-backed carpets are easier to work with than rubber-backed carpets.

Often carpet stores sell leftover ends very cheaply. Some times they are even given away. Obviously, it is easier to find remnants for smaller bulletin boards than for larger ones.

Fabrics can also make an excellent background, since they can be used over and over without showing puncture marks from pins or staples. Woven fabrics work out better than stretch fabrics, since they retain their shape and won't easily be snagged by pins or staples. The same considerations given to wallpaper choices also apply to fabric choices. Backgrounds will be most effective if limited to subtle stripes, single-colored textures, and tiny prints of things occurring in nature. Again color choices should be subtle.

Woven cotton fabrics are ideal for bulletin board backgrounds because they are relatively inexpensive and come in a rainbow of colors. The pastels usually not available in rolls of bulletin board paper are readily available in woven cottons. (Old sheets are easy to use and economical.) The currently popular calico prints may be suitable for some backgrounds. However, care must be taken to put the emphasis on God's message. Many religious themes do not lend themselves well to the "cute and cozy" look.

Fabric remnants are familiar items on sale tables. When purchasing fabrics to be used for bulletin board backgrounds, remember that fabrics are sold by the yard. (Cotton usually runs 45″ wide.) Be sure to figure your bulletin board measurements accordingly.

Another fabric that is an all-time favorite bulletin board background is burlap. Because of its coarse weave, burlap shows practically no wear, even after years of use. (Fading might be the only problem.) Burlap is usually sold by the yard and comes in a roll 60″ wide. It is usually wise to purchase burlap in a variety store rather than at an arts and crafts store, since it is generally less expensive. Burlap is available in a variety of colors, but the colors often tend to be somewhat dark and drab. Be sure that the color you select is appropriate for the message you wish to project.

Felt also makes a good bulletin board background but is generally quite expensive. If you are fortunate enough to find a good sale, remember that felt is sold by the yard and usually runs 60″ wide.

Drapery and upholstery fabric may also be used for effective bulletin boards. Again care must be taken to select simple designs in one basic color. Since these fabrics come in a variety of weights, be sure to select a relatively light-weight material. (One disadvantage of both drapery and upholstery fabric is that, because of their weight, they tend to droop or sag when spread across a large bulletin board.)

These fabrics are probably the least used as bulletin board backgrounds because of their weight and their expense. However, don't forget the possibility that garage sales may prove an inexpensive source of lightweight drapery fabric.

The use of the three basic background materials—paper, carpet, and fabric—are limited only by one's imagination. The same backgrounds (once cut to fit a specific bulletin board) can serve in many ways. When combined with a variety of letters, borders, and symbols, they can take on a "whole new look."

Borders

Many people feel that a bulletin board does not have a truly "finished" look unless it has a border. Certainly bulletin boards created for the glory of God should be as professional-looking as possible.

Effective border patterns are endless. Several school supply companies have ready-made border patterns on the market, however border patterns are not difficult to create. Just be sure your choices follow these basic rules:

Border patterns must be compatible with the letter patterns and with the background in both design and color. (For example, a geometric foil border on a burlap background with gothic lettering would be very incongruous; while a rather simply designed carpet border with carpet letters would be very harmonious with a burlap background.)

Border patterns and letter patterns need not necessarily be color-matched, but usually look better when cut from the same kind of material.

Strip Borders are made by laying a tagboard pattern on fabric or paper, tracing lightly with pencil or chalk, and cutting.

Paper strip borders are the easiest and quickest to make since three or four strips of paper can be cut at once. Many kinds of paper can be used, just as for backgrounds. In fact, there is more freedom for using prints, geometric designs, stripes, etc., in borders because smaller amounts are needed for borders and letters than for backgrounds. Wallpaper and gift-wrap designs too bold for a background may be just right for borders and letters.

Fabric strip borders should be cut singly, since layers of fabric tend to slip and slide, thus making the border uneven. The fabric chosen for border patterns should be heavier than the fabric selected for the background. (Felt, drapery, and upholstery fabrics are especially good, since they don't ravel, are easy to cut, and hold their shape without an excessive amount of pins or staples. Since only long, narrow strips of fabric are required, drooping and sagging doesn't usually become a problem.)

Strip borders made from carpeting are generally difficult to cut. If carpet is used, don't try a fancy border. Instead, cut a continual 1" to 1¼" strip of carpet for each side of the bulletin board. While this is not a fancy border, it is interesting because the raised texture of the carpet creates a "framed" look.

To use the following border patterns most efficiently, transfer each pattern to a piece of tagboard and then cut the pattern out. As the need arises, the patterns will be ready to trace onto paper or fabric. Meanwhile look for a long, narrow box in which to store these patterns.

Folded border patterns may be made by folding paper (accordian style), cutting as indicated on the pattern, and unfolding—just as if cutting a string of paper dolls.

Construction paper is one of the best materials for a folded border. However, gift wrap, wallpaper, foil, and other paper materials can also be used. Since there are "open" areas in this type of border, thus creating a see-through effect, solid colors should be used. Prints, stripes, or other designs tend to be too distracting when used with these patterns.

Some fabrics also lend themselves well to folded borders. Heavier fabrics such as felt, drapery, and upholstery fabrics are best for this purpose. Extreme care should be taken when folding and cutting to insure an evenly sized border.

8

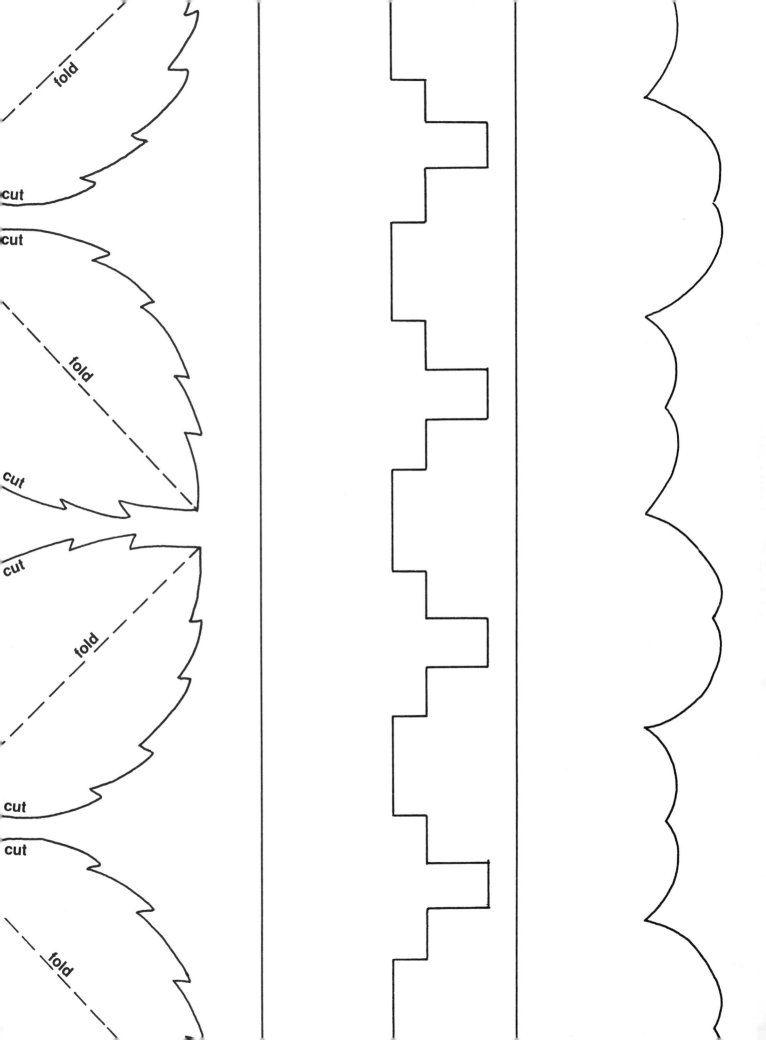

How to Make Folded Borders

Cut four strips of paper or fabric 1½" to 2" wide and as long as each side of the bulletin board. (If the material you wish to use is not long enough, cut several shorter pieces and splice them together as you pin the border to the bulletin board.)

Fold the strips (accordian style) back and forth. The folded piece should be the width of the pattern you wish to use.

Cut as indicated on the pattern.

Open to reveal the connected pieces.

Pin or staple along edges of the bulletin board.

Several border patterns follow. Again to make them durable and easy to use, they should be transfered to tagboard and cut out. As they are needed, they will be ready to use. It should be possible to store these patterns along with the "Strip Border" patterns.

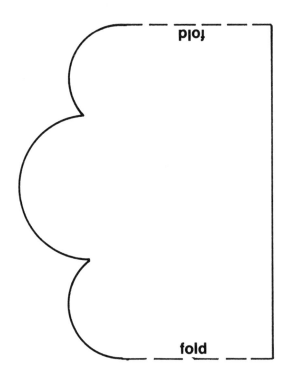

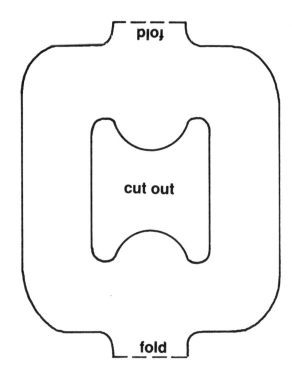

Single Piece Borders

Borders of single pieces repeated in a definite order—are also effective. These may be slightly more time consuming to mount, since they are pinned or stapled one piece at a time.

Ready-made pieces that are suitable for bulletin board borders may be found nearly everywhere. Consider a few of the following:

• Pine cones (thoroughly dried and free of pitch) are fine for harvest, Christmas, or winter themes.
• Dried flowers work well for harvest themes. (Spraying with hair spray after they are thoroughly dried helps to bring out the color.)
• Plastic or silk flowers are especially effective for Easter and Trinity themes. (Don't forget the possibility of coating old and fading flowers with gold spray paint for a very striking border.)

Many other household and classroom items may be used as borders as long as they are lightweight enough and thin enough to pin or staple to a bulletin board.

If desired, self-made pieces for bulletin board borders can be made easily from paper. Almost any shape can be used, but the shape must be in keeping with the theme of the bulletin board: Lillies for Easter or spring; leaves for harvest or Trinity; stars for Christmas or Epiphany; poinsettias for Christmas; crosses for Lent; etc.

Several single-piece border patterns follow. On any given board one pattern in a single color may be used or two or three colors and patterns may be combined. It is best to avoid using more than two colors or patterns on any one board. The pieces should be arranged symmetrically to create a finished look.

13

These single-piece borders may be used with one or both of the center inserts. The total look is more effective if both inserts are used in contrasting colors.

Most of the inserts are interchangeable, since the flower patterns are nearly the same size.

Any one or a combination of these flowers may be used alone or with the leaf patterns shown on page 15.

For a 3-D effect, crease each leaf lengthwise and pin in the crease.

leaf
pattern

leaf
pattern

leaf
pattern

Lettering

Letter patterns should always be compatible with the age of the viewer. For adults and older children, use all capitals in a decorative design. For younger children, use very plain upper and lowercase letters. There are many ready-made letter patterns marketed by a wide variety of companies.

The alphabet patterns that follow are suitable for bulletin boards that will be viewed by various age groups. All except perhaps the very young should be able to read the words made from these patterns.

These letter patterns will be easiest to use if transfered to tagboard and cut out. For efficient storage, cut strips of tagboard and tape them inside a gift box to create a section for each letter or pair of letters. Label each section with a marker.

As with borders, letters may be cut from construction paper, gift wrap, foil, carpet, etc. (Since carpet is difficult to cut, it should be used for very short messages cut from simple patterns.) If prints or other designs are used, it may be wise to outline each letter with a marker to insure readability. Cutting two letters each of contrasting colors and glueing them together in a slightly offset manner can also create an interesting effect.

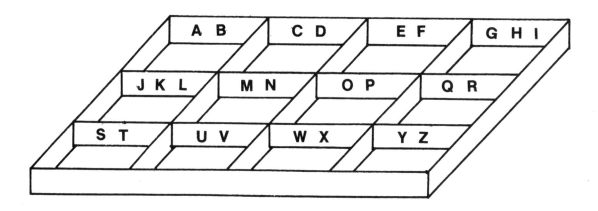

ABCDE

FGHIJK

LMNOP

QRSTU

VWXYZ

ABCD

EFGH

IJKL

MNO

P Q R S

T U V

W X Y

Z

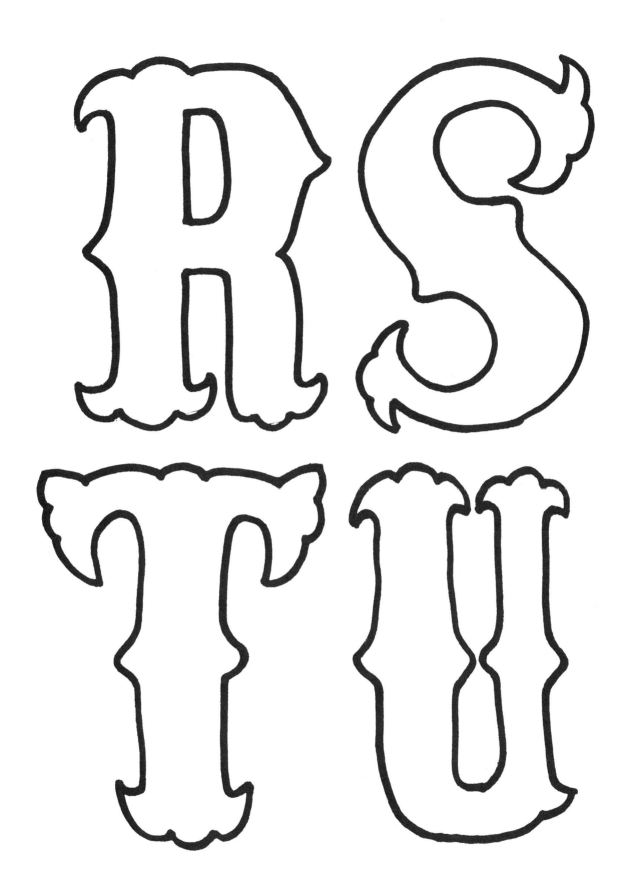

How to Proceed

Once you have an idea, sketch it—complete with borders, captions, etc. then—

A. Be flexible:
1. Try using several letter patterns until one seems best;
2. Try arranging the letters in a variety of ways until one way seems most effective;
3. Try several border patterns until one seems to be most compatible with the other elements of the board;
4. Try using a variety of materials—not for a "sensational" effect, but to strive for the combination that best brings out God's message.
B. Be precise:
1. Select letter and border patterns which project sincerity (God's Word is not to be taken lightly);
2. Use colors which best stress the ideas being presented—
   a. Green for Christian growth;
   b. Blue for loyalty;
   c. Red for salvation through the blood of Christ;
   d. Yellow for Christ, the Light of the world;
   e. Black for sin and transgression;
   f. White for purity and righteousness.
3. Use bold dramatic colors and textures to present bold and dramatic ideas; use pastels and softer textures to present love, gentleness, etc.
4. Use symbols that are scripturally sound, even though they may not be "artistically correct"; make sure that the symbols project ideas rather than merely adding decorations. (After all, not everyone will read the caption: make sure they get a message, even at a glance.)
5. Do all cutting, painting, drawing, glueing, etc., with the greatest of care. (Extra time taken on God's bulletin board is never wasted!)

The Final Touch

Once the last letter has been cut, the last pin put in place, and the last scrap picked up, there is but one thing left to do: thank the Lord for this opportunity to serve Him and pray that all who will see His Word portrayed will receive the message He intended.

God's Blessings!

Feed My Lambs

This bulletin board is especially suitable for the beginning of the school year, the Sunday school year, or vacation Bible school. It is also ideal for a general theme of nurturing the young with the milk of God's Holy Word. With this in mind, it may be used for the installation of day school or Sunday school teachers, Sunday school superintendents, board of education members, etc.

The number of the lambs can vary, depending on the size of the bulletin board or whether it is intended for a class of a specific size. If a small number of children are involved in the class, their names could be written on the lambs.

Suggested Color Scheme

Background: red.

Border and letters: yellow calico print wrapping paper.

Lambs: white, outlined with black marker.

Bible: black cover with gold foil page edges and white open page (calligraphy would be very effective for the printing). See the "Open Bible" instructions on page 57 for help in constructing the Bible.

Let Us in Grace and Wisdom

This caption, taken from the familiar hymn, "Abide, O Dearest Jesus," recognizes the true Source of all wisdom. The roots of the tree draw their nourishment from the four gospels.

This design is suitable for the beginning of the day school or Sunday school year, for a series of Bible classes, or for the Trinity season—our season of growth.

The tree (cut from green and brown carpet) can serve as a symbol on many other bulletin boards. For example, red "fruit" or "fruit" of assorted shapes and sizes (made from construction paper) can be labeled with the seven fruits of the Spirit and attached to the tree or "Only God Can Make a Tree" can be used as a caption on another board that shows our thankfulness for God's creation.

Suggested Color Scheme

Tree top: green carpet.

Tree trunk: brown carpet.

Caption letters: brown carpet.

Gospel letters: brown construction paper.

Border: green leaves cut from patterns shown on page 13.

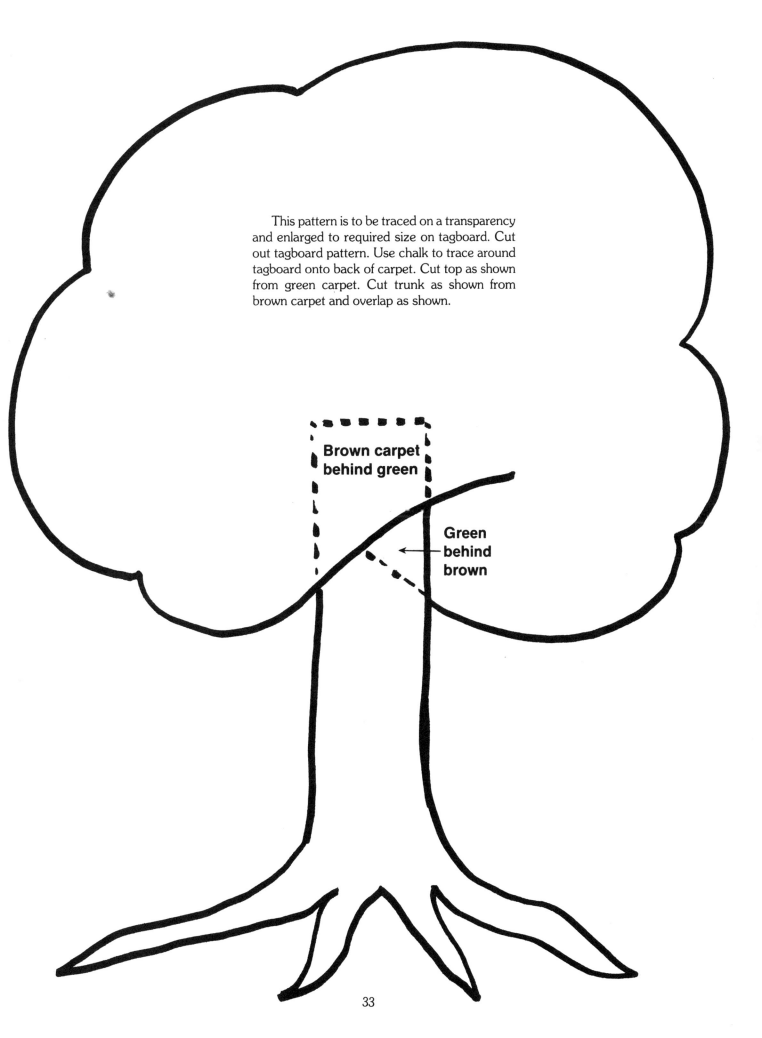

This pattern is to be traced on a transparency and enlarged to required size on tagboard. Cut out tagboard pattern. Use chalk to trace around tagboard onto back of carpet. Cut top as shown from green carpet. Cut trunk as shown from brown carpet and overlap as shown.

Brown carpet behind green

Green behind brown

October

"This Is the Day
Which the Lord
Has Made;
Let Us Rejoice
and Be Glad in It."

Ps. 118:24

This Is the Day

The beauty of God's creation is especially evident in autumn. The black trees serve as a frame to create a "framed window" effect.

These trees, once cut to fit a bulletin board, can be used in many ways:

In midwinter the trees can be left bare, and white hillside cut to represent snow; then add a few sparrows with the verse from Matt. 10:29.

For Thanksgiving use the black trees with autumn leaves and a green hillside; add ready-made pilgrim figures, with Eph. 5:20 printed on a scroll in the center.

Suggested Color Scheme

Trees: black bulletin board paper. (This is easier to work with than several pieces of smaller construction paper.) Be sure to cut two trees and reverse one to get a right and a left. (For efficient storage, wrap trees around the cardboard core from a roll of gift wrap.)

Hillsides: green bulletin board paper, textured fabric, or carpet. No pattern should be required: Simply measure about one-third of the way up the side of the bulletin board to get the height, and cut shapes similar to those on page 35. (Overlap when pinning for a more realistic effect.)

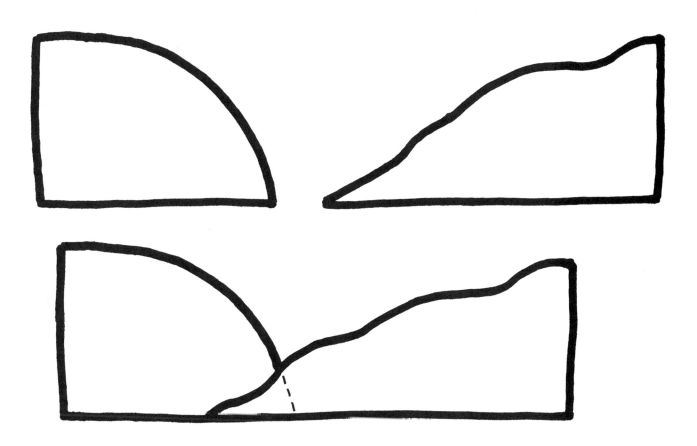

If desired, the pattern on this page may be traced onto a transparency and enlarged to fit a specific bulletin board.

Leaves: construction paper of yellow, gold, orange, red, green, and brown. (See pattern on page 36—the oak leaf pattern is best suited for this purpose because of its size and shape.)

Sun: yellow construction paper. (Use any round object of desired size as a half circle pattern—kettle cover, pizza pan, etc.)

Letters: black construction paper cut from a simple letter pattern (since there are quite a few words in the caption).

Tree Border: the pattern on this page can be traced onto a transparency and enlarged to the desired size on tagboard. Then use chalk to trace the tagboard pattern onto black bulletin board paper. (Be sure to cut two trees and reverse one to get a right and a left.)

The top branch may need to be extended so that right and left trees meet at the center of the bulletin board. (This will depend on the width of the bulletin board.)

If a small bulletin board will be used, the leaf pattern here might be of a better proportion than the one on page 13.

36

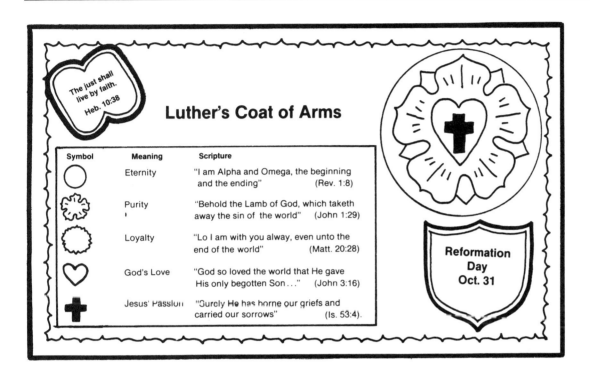

Luther's Coat of Arms

An explanation of the symbolism used in Luther's coat of arms is the focus of this bulletin board.

Luther's shield is shown in its entirety. The effect is best if each part is made separately and then glued together in layers. Be sure to cover it with books or similar heavy objects to prevent curling while it is drying.

Luther's shield is also shown piece by piece, each complete with its meaning and a supporting Scripture verse. These smaller symbols need only to be drawn on a piece of tagboard and colored with markers. Be sure to provide a sufficient amount of lines (lightly penciled in) to allow for all the printing required. The printing should be done with a permanent marker to avoid smearing during construction, display, or storage.

Suggested Color Scheme
Background: blue bulletin board paper.
Outer circle: gold foil mounted on tagboard.
Heart: red tagboard.
Cross: black construction paper.
Open Bible: see instructions on page 57.
Border: white construction paper.
Letters: black or white construction paper.

This pattern is to be traced onto a transparency and enlarged onto tagboard to desired size.

Depending on the size of the bulletin board, this shield may be used as it is, or enlarged slightly.

Outer layer: black construction paper.
Middle layer: gold foil.
Inner layer: white typing paper.

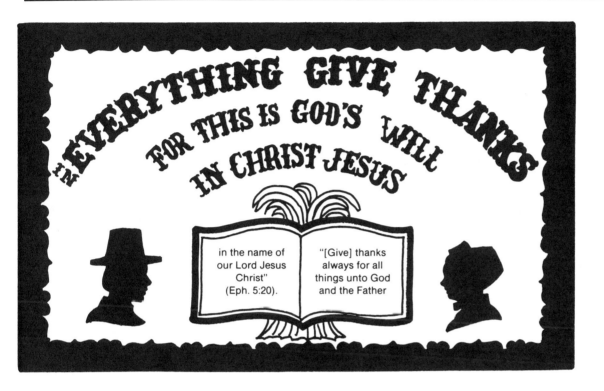

In Everything Give Thanks

Pilgrim silhouettes look to Scripture for their strength. A shock of real wheat pinned behind the open Bible can serve as a reminder of our real Bread of life, Jesus Christ. (Ready-made cornshocks are available from most school supply stores in autumn if real wheat is not readily available.)

Suggested Color Scheme

Background: gold foil. (If this is not available, yellow bulletin board paper may be substituted.)

Borders: black construction paper.

Letters: black construction paper.

Silhouettes: black construction paper.

Open Bible: see instructions on page 57. (The gold foil layer may be omitted if a gold foil background is used.)

This pattern may be used as it is, or it may be transferred to a transparency and enlarged to the desired size.

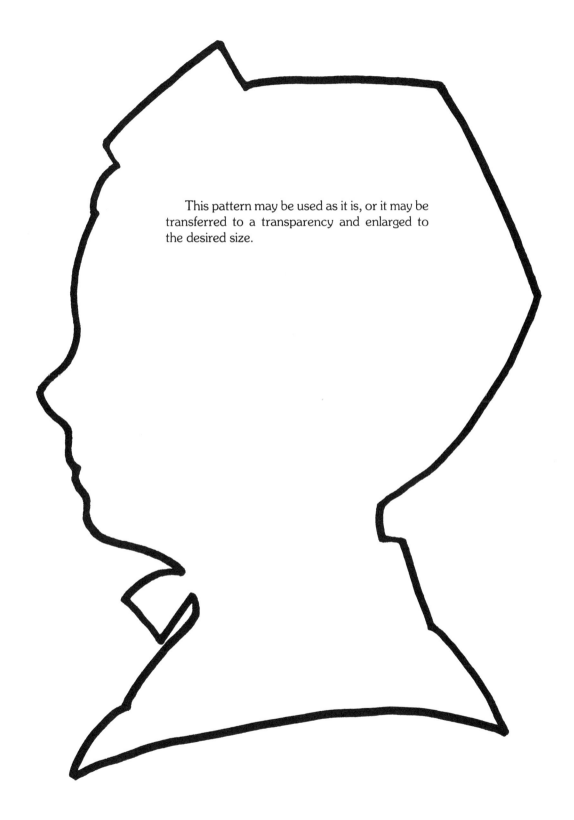

This pattern may be used as it is, or it may be transferred to a transparency and enlarged to the desired size.

Thank God for Promises Kept

A subtle pastel rainbow symbolizes God's promises to man. The black trees serve to frame the basic truths of John 3:16.

Each of the phrases is printed on a ribbonlike banner. Above the banners a symbol for each idea is displayed.

Suggested Color Scheme

Background: light blue bulletin board paper on which a watercolor rainbow has been painted. (Be sure to paint the rainbow while the paper is flat on the floor to prevent the colors from running.)

Trees: black construction paper. See pattern on page 36.

Border: black construction paper (bottom only).

Banners: white construction paper.

Stable and manger: black construction paper with gold foil rays radiating from the infant's head.

Crosses: black construction paper.

Crown of thorns: brown construction paper.

Crown of glory: gold foil with sequins, rhinestones, etc.

(For the "Easter" cross use white plastic flowers to create a 3-D effect. Tiny flowers work best and are most effective if some greens are included.)

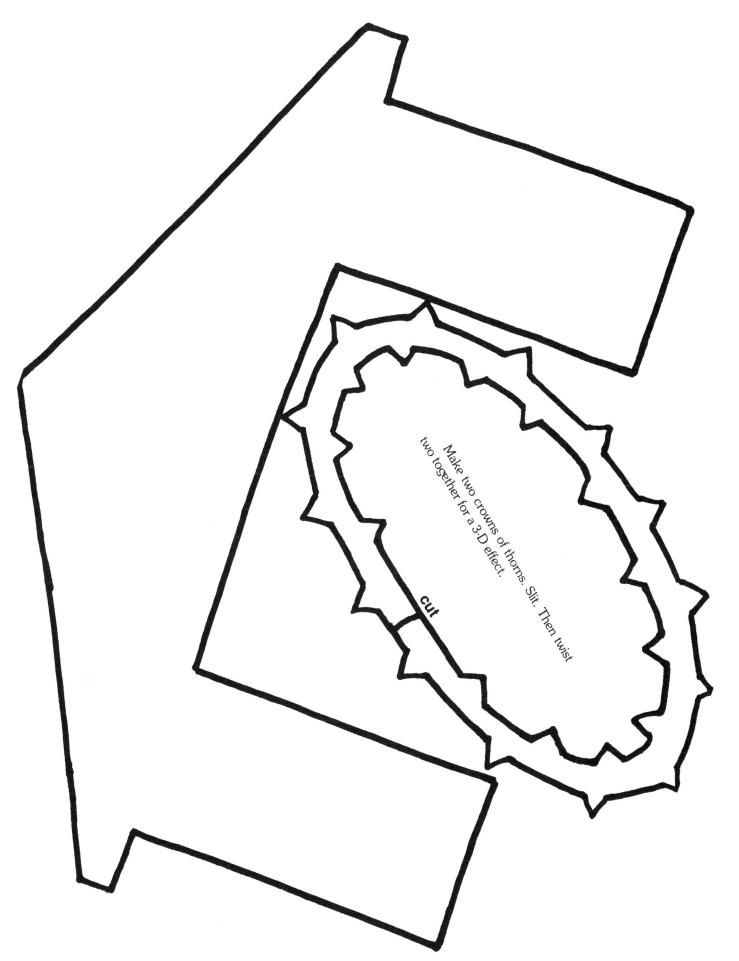

Make two crowns of thorns. Slit. Then twist two together for a 3-D effect.

cut

Each cross is made with one piece of black construction paper 1¼″ x 14″ and another piece 1¼″ x 7″.

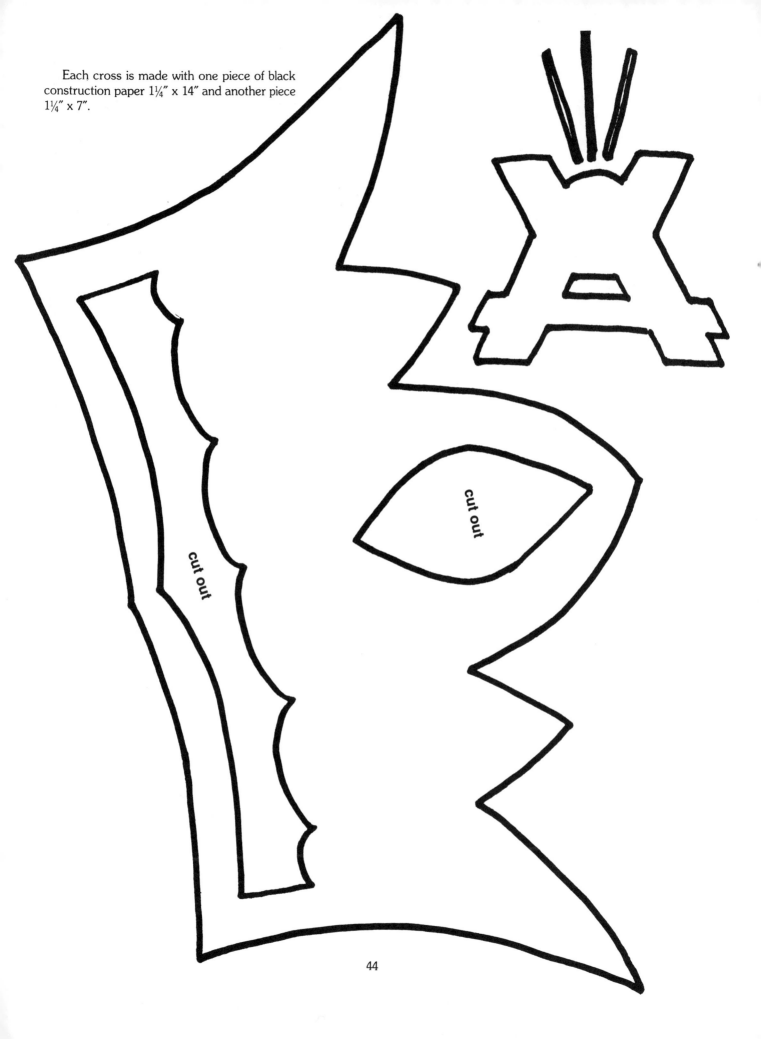

cut out

cut out

44

All of these patterns pertaining to "Thank God for Promises Kept" are scaled for a bulletin board approximately 3′ x 5′. If the board to be used is significantly larger or smaller than this, the patterns will have to be adjusted accordingly.

The "banners" cut from white construction paper may need to be made larger or smaller, depending on the size of the bulletin board. This is easily done by adjusting the fold line (upward for smaller; downward for larger).

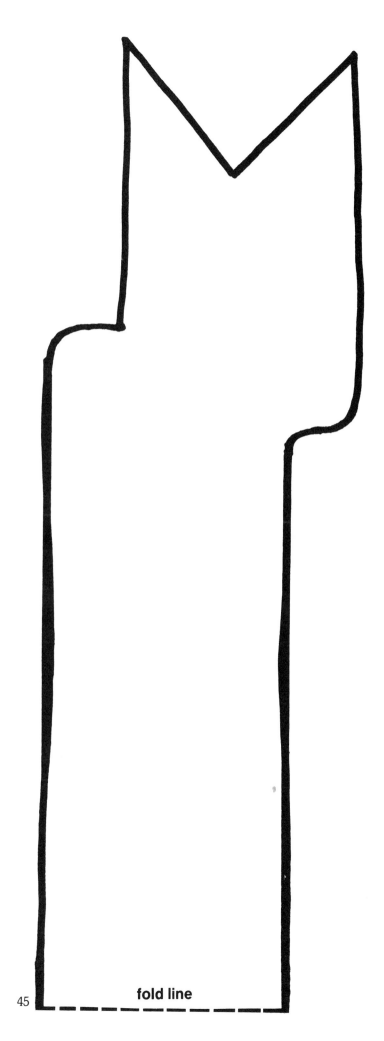

fold line

Peace on Earth

The dove of peace carries an olive branch as the angels' Christmas message is announced.

This board provides an excellent opportunity to try your hand at creating your own stylized letter patterns similar to those shown here. Otherwise, any of the letter patterns shown in this book will work well. Your choice will depend only on the size of the bulletin board.

Suggested Color Scheme

Background: royal blue bulletin board paper.
Border and letters: white construction paper.

Dove: white typing paper (The farther wing is pinned flat to the bulletin board, as is the body. The closer wing is slit and overlapped to create an "off-center cone shape." When pinned over the body in this way, the wing will have a 3-D look. White quilling paper may be used for the extended lines.)

Leaves: white construction paper (For a 3-D effect, fold each leaf in half lengthwise and pin in the center.) Arrange the leaves along the stem with the largest at the bottom and the smallest at the top.

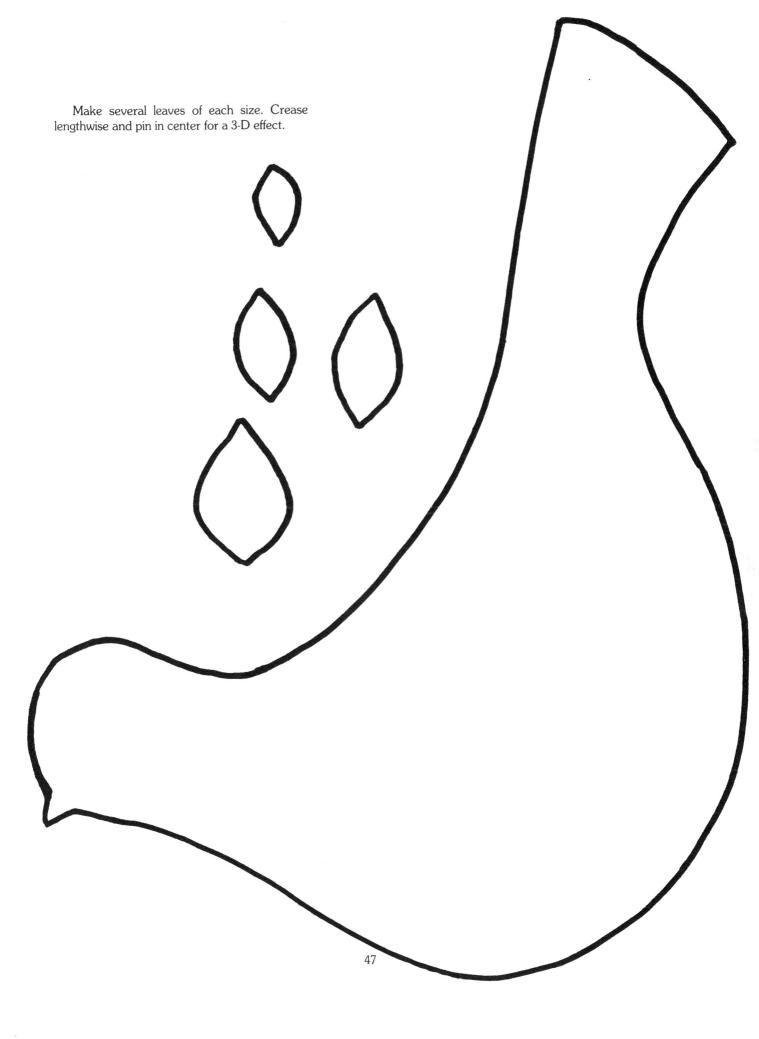

Make several leaves of each size. Crease
lengthwise and pin in center for a 3-D effect.

Cut two wings. Pin farther wing flat to board.
Cut slit in closer wing, and pin so that A and B
overlap for a 3-D effect.

B A

48

Chrismons—Symbols of Our Faith

This bulletin board is educational as well as inspirational. Each Chrismon is shown in its actual size on the tree. It is then shown again in miniature on a card which explains the meaning of the symbol.

Suggested Color Scheme:
Background: bright red bulletin board paper.
Border and letters: white construction paper.

Chrismons: white tagboard with gold foil and gold glitter as indicated on each pattern.
Tree: green carpet. (Indoor-outdoor carpet is excellent!)

Tree Pattern
This pattern can be traced onto a transparency and enlarged to desired size on tagboard. After tagboard has been cut out, trace with chalk onto back of carpet and cut.

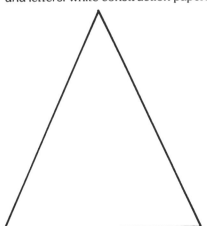

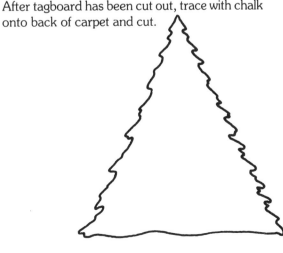

51

The Chi Rho and the Sun. The letters *Chi* (X) and *Rho* (P) are the first two letters of Christ's name in Greek (*XPICTOC*—pronounced "Christos"). This symbol, which is an abbreviation of Christ's name, is one of the oldest and most familiar of all Christian symbols. The sun is a Messianic symbol of our Lord and recalls the prophecy in Mal. 4:2, where Jesus is called the "Sun of righteousness."

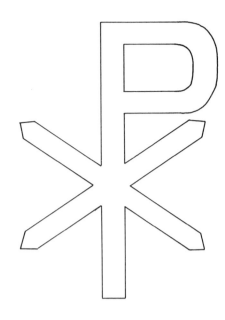

Christ—the Cornerstone. Christ is the Cornerstone of the church. Different forms of His name appear on each face of the stone.

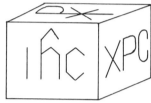

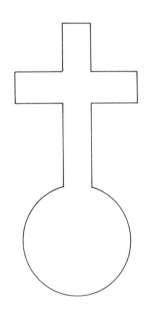

The Cross and the Sphere. This Chrismon is traditionally called the Cross of Triumph or the Cross of Victory. It is a symbol of the triumphant and glorified Lord. The sphere represents the entire world. The cross symbolizes Christ's triumph over the sin of the world.

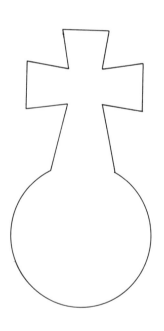

The Jerusalem Cross. Crusaders emblazoned this cross on their shields. It is also known as the Fivefold Cross and the Crusader's Cross. The five crosses of this Chrismon symbolize the five wounds of our Lord, as well as the nations of Europe that participated in the Crusades: Italy, Spain, France, Germany, and Great Britain. The four Tau crosses which comprise the large cross symbolize the Old Testament prophecies of a Savior. The four small crosses represent the spread of the Gospel to the four corners of the world.

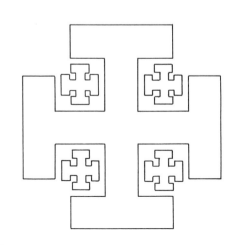

The Greek Cross. The Greek Cross has four arms of equal length. This Greek cross, with a crown at the end of each arm, symbolizes our Lord's kingship and His victory over sin and death. The sun behind the cross recalls the glory of the victorious Christ, the Messiah.

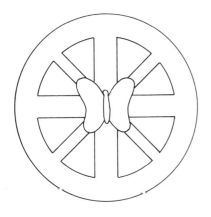

The Greek Cross with Chi. *Chi* (X) is the first letter of Christ's name in Greek. The circle symbolizes eternity; the cross, Christ's atonement for our sins. The butterfly represents the Resurrection and reminds us of the new life we have in Christ.

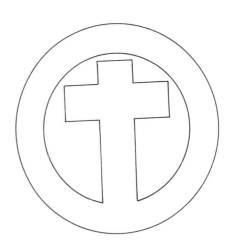

The Roman, or Latin, Cross. This cross is universally recognized by all Christians as the symbol of the atoning death of Jesus our Savior. Here the cross is combined with Alpha (the first letter of the Greek alphabet) and Omega (the last letter of the Greek alphabet). These letters remind us that Christ is everything to us—from A to Z—from the beginning to the end.

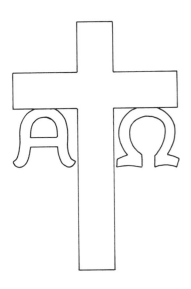

The Cross Within a Circle. The circle, having neither beginning nor end, symbolizes eternity. The cross, combined here with the circle, represents the complete and everlasting nature of Christ's work and kingdom.

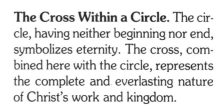

A Cross Patee with Scrolls. The graceful outward curve of its arms is the hallmark of the Cross Patee. Here the cross is combined with the circle of eternity and four scrolls, which represent the four evangelists —Matthew, Mark, Luke, and John, who reveal in their gospels the story of God's plan of salvation for man.

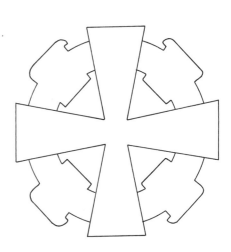

IHC. This symbol is formed from the first three letters of the Greek word for Jesus, *IHCOYC*. A variation, IHS, is also used. Together with the cross, IHC and IHS remind us that our ransom from sin and the devil was paid for by Christ's suffering and death on the cross.

The Tau Cross is a cross shaped like the Greek letter T, which is called *Tau*. This T-shaped cross is sometimes called the Old Testament Cross because it is said to have been the type of cross on which Moses placed the bronze snake (Num. 21:8-9; John 3:14). In Christian art, the thieves crucified with Christ are often depicted on Tau crosses.

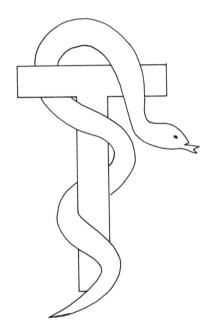

Three Entwined Circles. Three perfect circles, symbolizing the eternal nature of the three persons in the Trinity, have long been a familiar way to express the doctrine of the Trinity. The entwined circles show that there are three distinct Persons yet one eternal God.

IXOYC—Ichthus, or Fish. An acrostic used by early Christians. The letters *IXOYC* make up the Greek word for fish; they are also the first letters in Greek of "Jesus Christ, Son of God, Savior." This symbol was one of profound significance for the early Christian, testifying to eternal comfort and salvation found only in Jesus Christ.

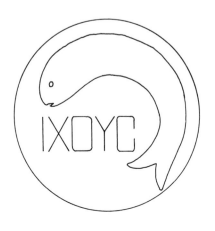

The Open Bible

The open Bible is often used in this collection of bulletin board ideas. However, no pattern is given, since the Bibles are of various sizes. It is an easy task to cut one's own pattern in the proper size.

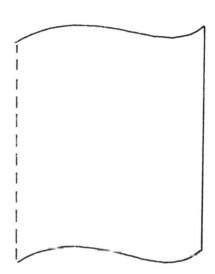

A. Decide on the size desired. Fold a piece of paper (a bit larger than desired size) in half. Draw a pattern similar to the one below.
B. Lay pattern on black construction paper and cut on all sides, except the fold.
C. Now, recut the pattern slightly smaller (½"—1½" smaller, depending on the size of the Bible).
D. Lay smaller pattern on bright red or gold foil paper and cut as above.
E. Then, recut pattern still smaller.
F. Lay the smallest pattern on white paper and cut as above.
G. Use a ruler to mark light lines for printing, and print the desired verse.
H. Lay the three pieces as shown, and pin to create an open book effect.

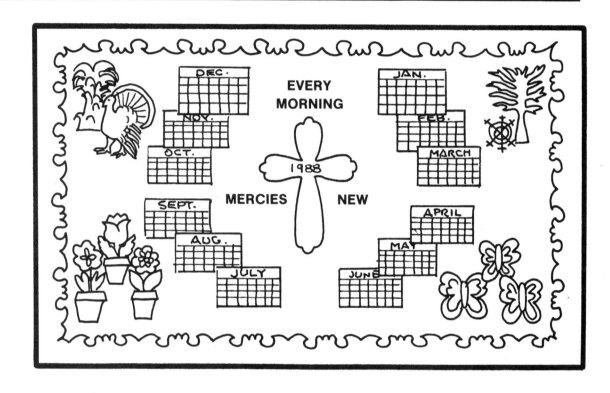

Every Morning Mercies New

God daily forgives and blesses our lives with a fresh new opportunity to live for His glory! A desk calendar, which has been taken apart and arranged in groups of three months, represents the four seasons. The symbols of each season represent our Father's earthly gifts to us.

Suggested Color Scheme

Background: light green or light blue bulletin board paper.

Border and Letters: dark green, dark blue, or black construction paper.

Central Cross: black w/gold numbers or gold w/black numbers.

Tree: black construction paper.

Snowflake: white typing paper.

Butterflies:
Flowers: } white construction paper colored with liquid markers.
Turkey:
Cornshock:

B

A

B A Overlap

Make two flower pots

A Overlap B

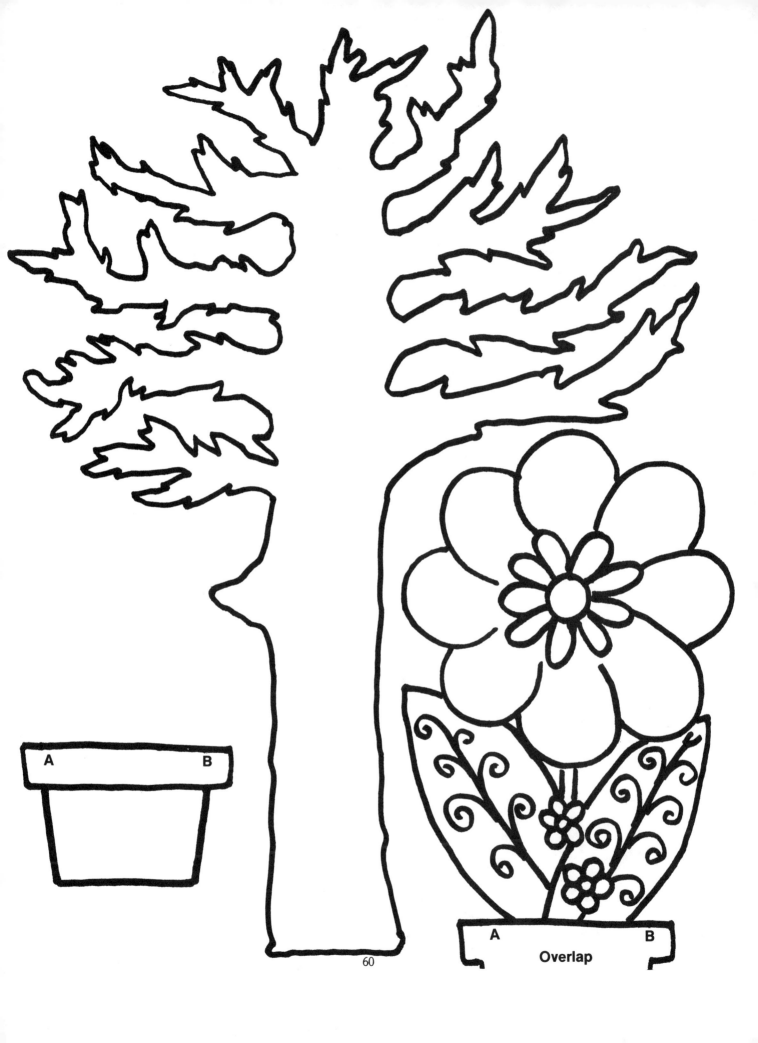

A   B

A   B   Overlap

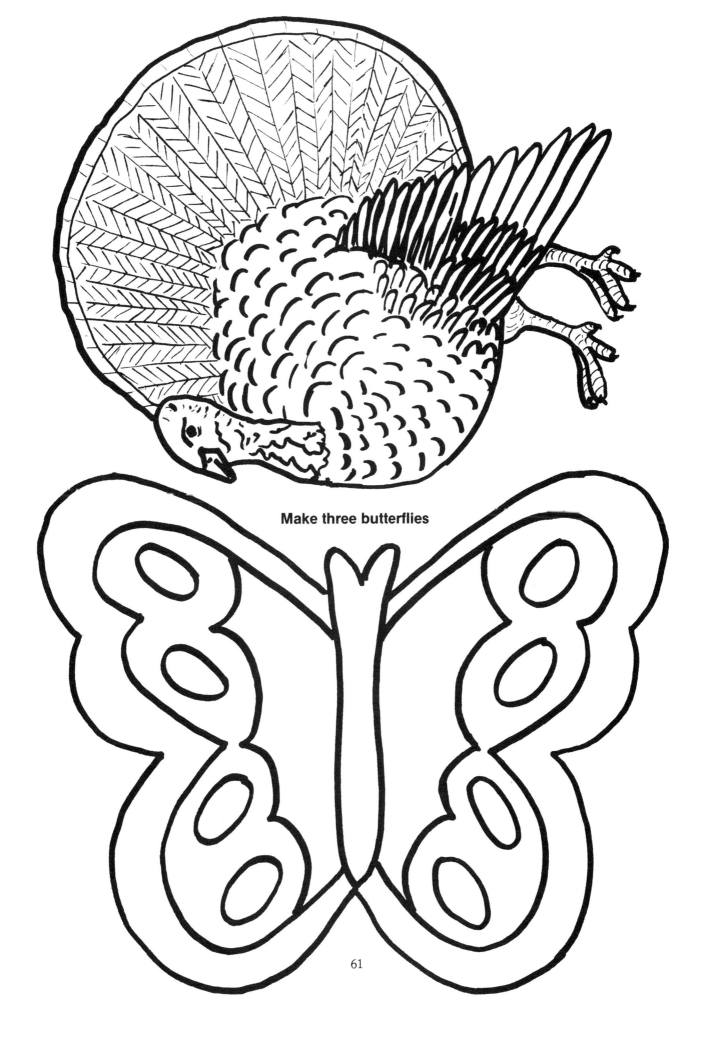

Make three butterflies

61

Let the Spirit Lead You—

The theme of every new year should be submission to the Holy Spirit's guidance. This main idea could also be used for Pentecost, for opening of the school year, or for graduation. (The words "in 19—" would then be eliminated.)

Suggested Color Scheme

Background: royal blue bulletin board paper or fabric.

Border and letters: white construction paper.

Tongue of Fire: red, orange, gold and yellow construction paper.

Dove: white construction paper.

Olive branch: dark green construction paper. (For a 3-D effect, crease each leaf lengthwise and pin in the crease. Arrange along the stem.)

Open Bible: see instructions on page 57.

Tassel bookmark: red braided yarn with hanging tassel.

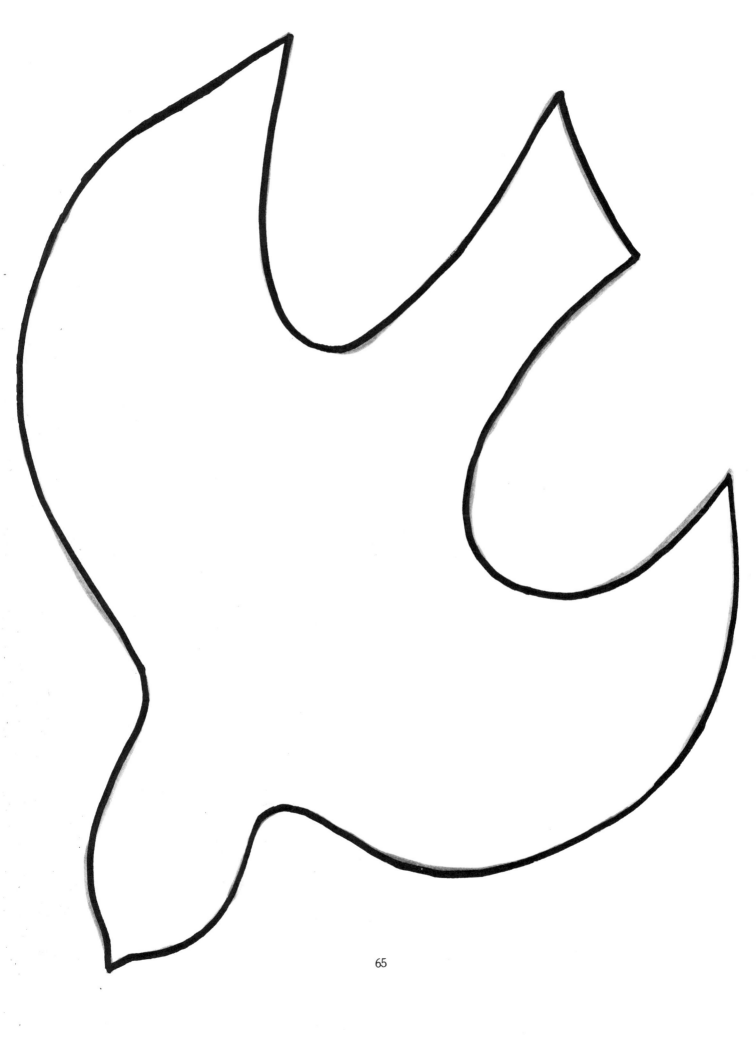

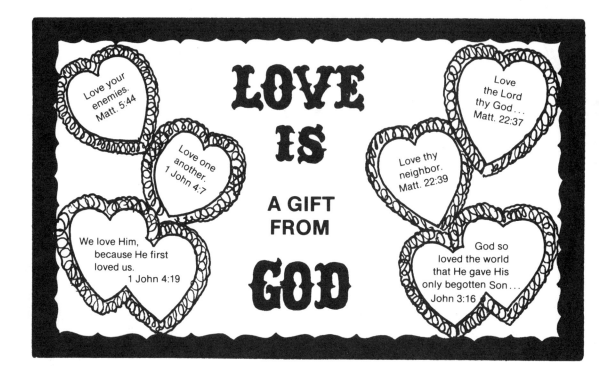

Love Is a Gift from God

Familiar "love" verses from Scripture remind all Christians that all love has God as its source. Notice that the words "LOVE IS GOD" are displayed in larger letters. An observant viewer will note that this is a reversal of the universally known Scripture verse "God is Love."

Suggested Color Scheme
Background: white bulletin board paper.
Border and Letters: red and gold "flocked" wallpaper (or any all-over design in a red wallpaper pattern).
Center Hearts: white construction paper.
Outer Hearts: ready-made heart-shaped lace doilies.

If a red background is used, borders, letters, and lace hearts should be white. (Borders and letters would then be effective if done in a white and gold patterned wallpaper.)

"Love is a Gift of God" pattern: print appropriate Bible verses on white hearts; fasten to ready-made red "lace" hearts.

There Is but One Perfect Love

A single large heart symbolizes God's love for his children. A black cross covered with white flowers reminds us of Christ's death upon the cross and His glorious resurrection. The red bow supporting the flowers has two streamers, each trimmed with a gold foil cross, thus representing the three crosses at Calvary.

Suggested Color Scheme

Background: red bulletin board paper.

Border and letters: white construction paper.

Flowers: white plastic or ready-made white silk flowers.

Bow with streamers: red ribbon with one gold foil cross attached to the end of each streamer.

Heart: see pattern on page 69.

Outer edge of heart: white paper lace doilies cut in half and arranged in a scallop design.

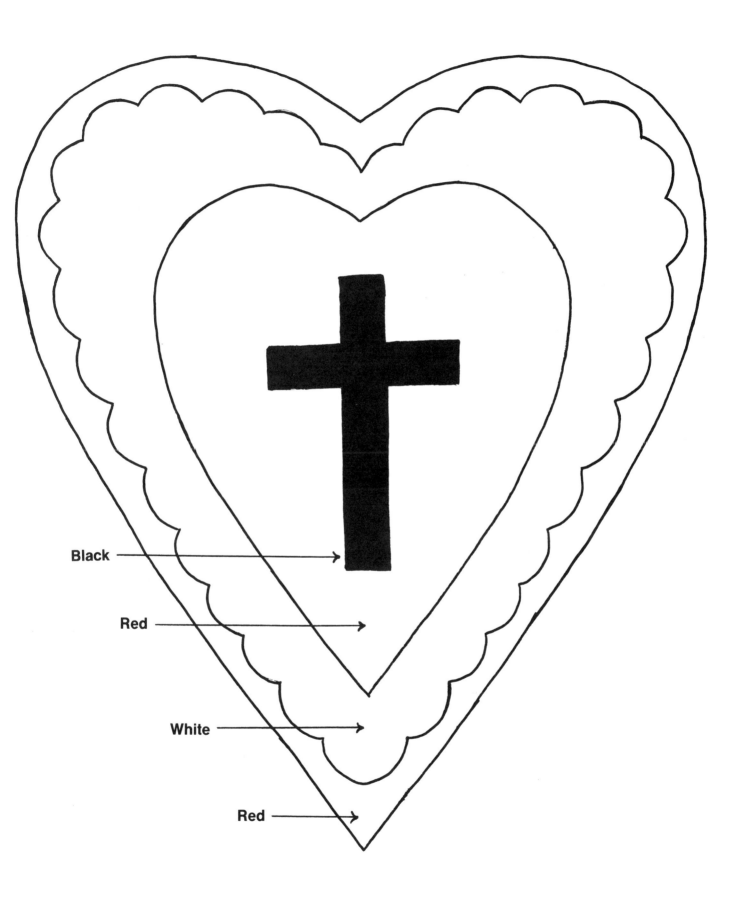

Black

Red

White

Red

"FOR THIS CAUSE
CAME [HE]
INTO THE WORLD..."

John 18:37

...THAT THE WORLD
THROUGH HIM
MIGHT BE SAVED.

John 3:17

For This Cause

Infant hands reach toward the cross, showing the purpose of Christ's birth and death. The entire scene can be traced onto a transparency and enlarged to the desired size by using an overhead projector. Then, watercolors can be used to paint this scene on a white background.

(This picture is taken from the Bethel Series. Copyright 1961, 1981, The Adult Christian Education Foundation. Used by permission.)

Suggested Color Scheme

Background: white tagboard (Two to four sheets of white tagboard should be enough to cover most bulletin board areas. Tape the sheets together carefully when tracing the pattern from the transparency.)

Border and letters: purple construction paper (For purposes of reuse during other Lenten seasons, it is best to glue the letters in place, thus saving time and making storage easy.)

Clouds: light blue watercolor around clouded areas.

Earth: green to represent land and blue to represent water.

Crown: gold foil glued over tagboard.

Manger: brown permanent marker (blanket should be left white).

Infant: skin-colored crayon and brown marker for hair.

Adult hands: skin-colored crayon.

Crown of thorns: brown permanent marker.

Cross: brown permanent marker with wood grain in black marker.

Rays of sunlight: yellow water color blended into light blue.

Trace onto transparency and use overhead projector to enlarge to desired size.

Given for You

The tiny drops of red blood are the focal point of this display. Although simple in design, this bulletin board inspires serious reflection on the meaning of Christ's death to every Christian. While this theme is most appropriate during the Lenten season, it is also very fitting anytime and anywhere the Lord's Supper is distributed. The clusters of grapes reinforce the concept of the Lord's Supper consisting of blood and wine, body and bread.

Suggested Color Scheme

Background: white bulletin board paper (wallpaper in an offwhite with a very subtle swirl design is also very effective).

Border and letters: purple construction paper.

Cross: black construction paper cut 3"—4" wide and as long as appropriate for a given area.

Crown of thorns: brown construction paper.

Clusters of grapes: white construction paper colored with liquid markers and covered with clear contact paper for a glossy effect.

Leaves: green construction paper creased in the center for a 3-D effect.

Vine: brown yarn coiled here and there as needed to fill in spaces between leaves.

Chalice and paten: gold foil. See pattern for details.

Cut one crown in a continuous oval. Cut a second crown and slit as marked (*). Twist the slitted crown around the solid crown for a 3-D effect.

*

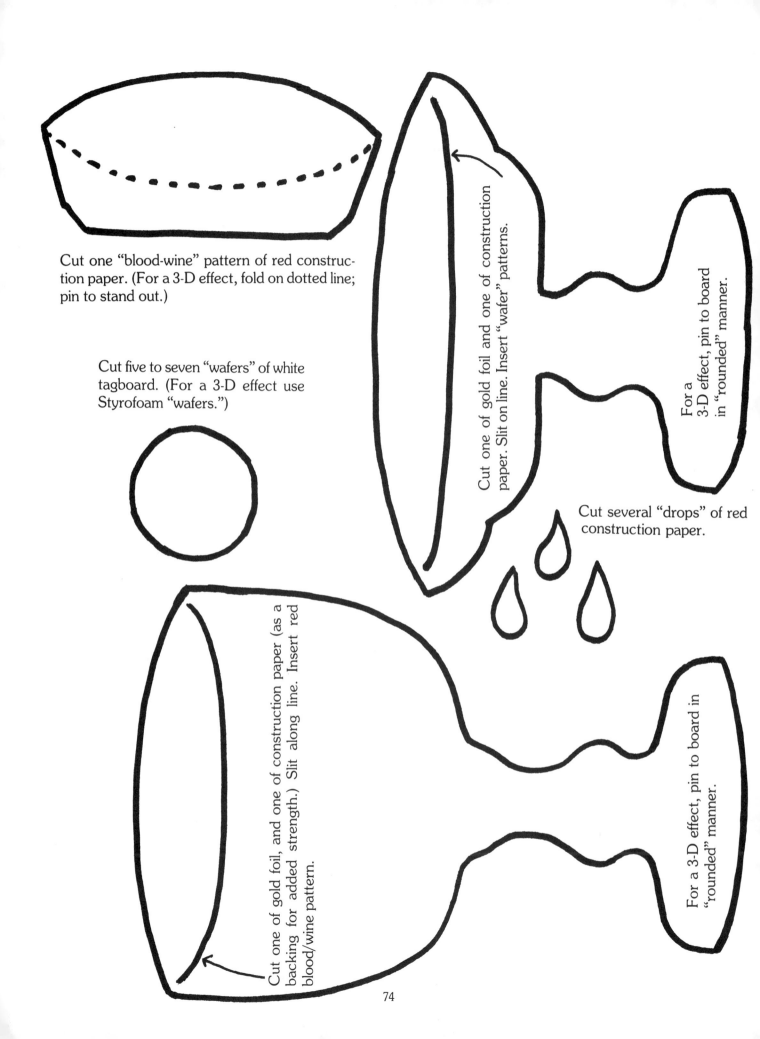

Cut one "blood-wine" pattern of red construction paper. (For a 3-D effect, fold on dotted line; pin to stand out.)

Cut five to seven "wafers" of white tagboard. (For a 3-D effect use Styrofoam "wafers.")

Cut one of gold foil and one of construction paper. Slit on line. Insert "wafer" patterns.

For a 3-D effect, pin to board in "rounded" manner.

Cut several "drops" of red construction paper.

Cut one of gold foil, and one of construction paper (as a backing for added strength.) Slit along line. Insert red blood/wine pattern.

For a 3-D effect, pin to board in "rounded" manner.

74

Crown Him with Many Crowns

This line from the famous Easter anthem symbolizes Christ's victory over death and the devil as well as Christ's gift of eternal life to us.

Suggested Color Scheme

Background: white bulletin board paper.

Border and Letters: purple construction paper.

Palm branches: green construction paper or real branches.

Crowns: gold foil with open areas to be filled with rich fabrics in royal colors (red, blue, green, or purple velvet). Rhinestones and other bits of jewelry may be used to trim the crowns.

If the crown patterns on the following pages need to be enlarged or made smaller to fit the bulletin board, trace them onto a transparency and then onto tagboard in desired size.

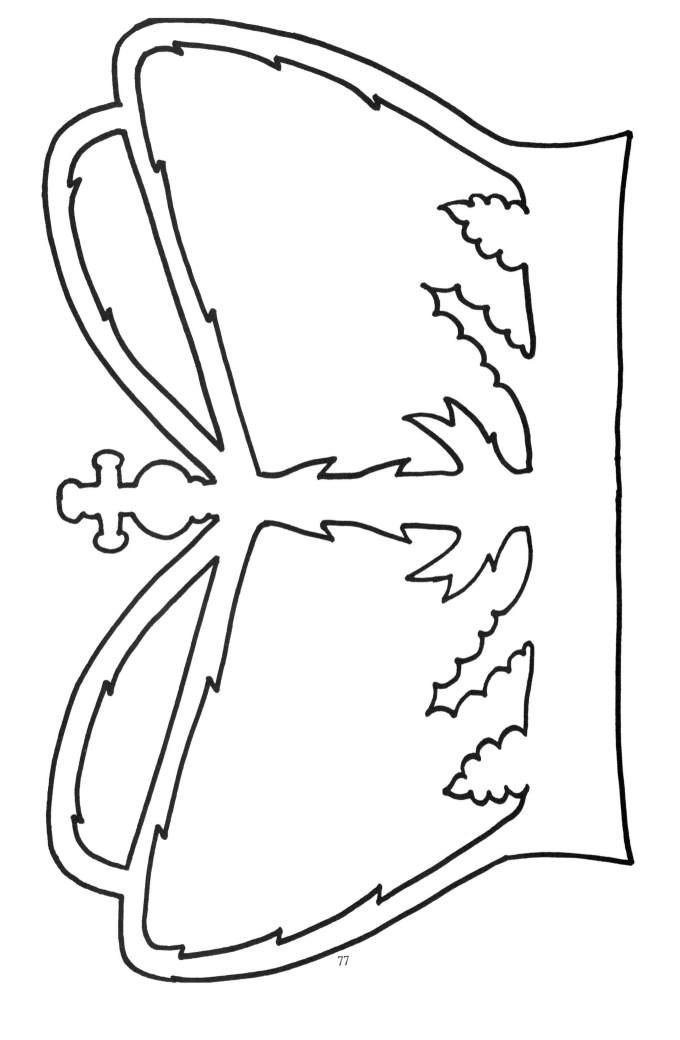

77

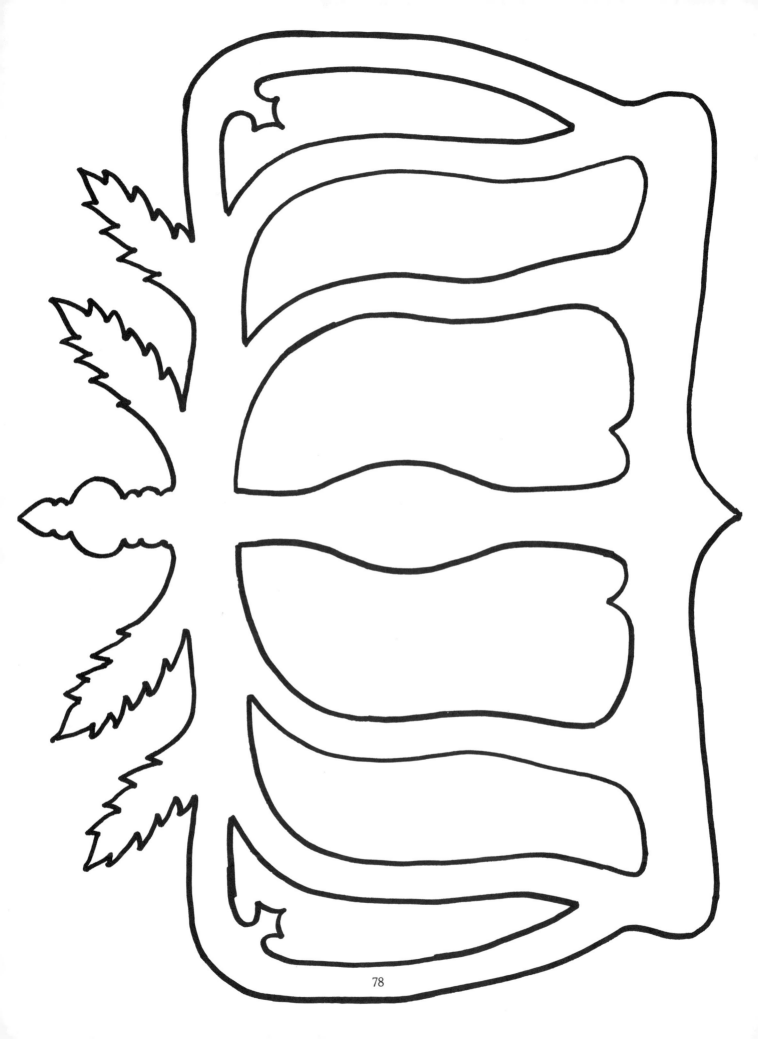

78

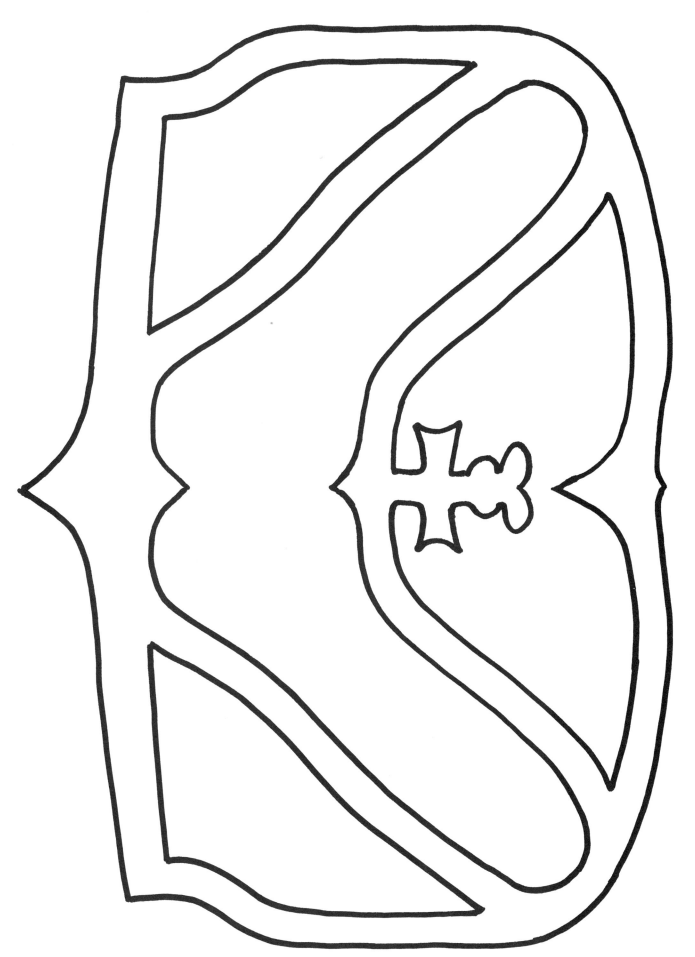

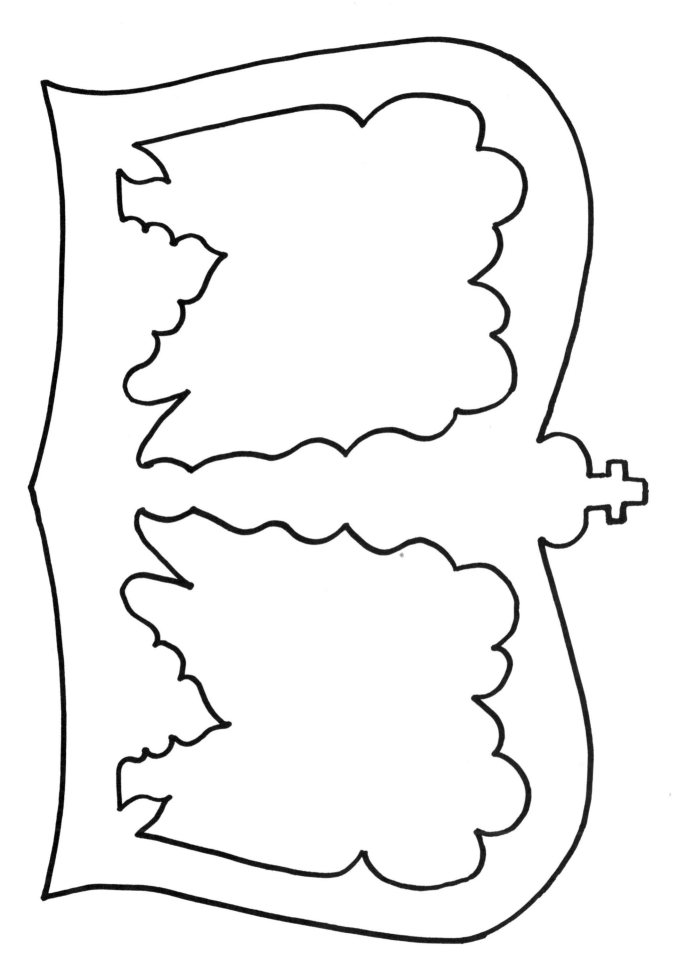

81

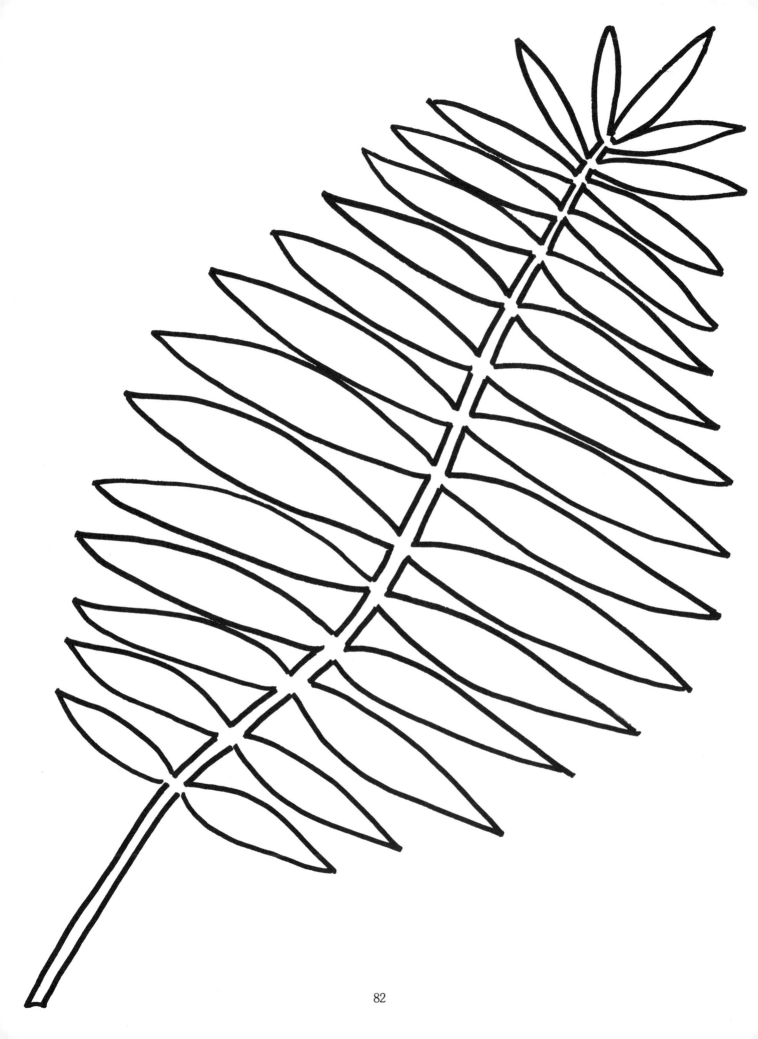

82

Because I Live

The traditional symbol of Easter is further enhanced by the brilliant yellow sunrise. The rays of the sun reaching to the perimeter of the board symbolize the spread of the Good News of salvation through faith. The flowers emphasize the message of new life.

Suggested Color Scheme
Background: white bulletin board paper.

Border and Letters: yellow construction paper outlined in black permanent marker.

Sunrise: yellow construction paper (preferably a shade or two darker than the letters and border).

Cross: brown construction paper, woodgrain wallpaper, or very thin strips of paneling.

Flowers: paper (see pattern on following page), plastic Easter lilies, or silk Easter lilies.

Come, Holy Spirit

The power of Pentecost should inspire awe in every Christian. This invitation to the Holy Spirit to fill our empty vessels could also be used at Baptisms, confirmations, etc.

To add interest to the three symbols shown, cut yarn of appropriate colors into ¼″ pieces. (Use red for the heart; red, orange, and gold for the flames; white for the dove.) Then, cover with glue brushed on thinly. Next, cover the wet glue with the shredded yarn. Pat it down lightly. Allow to dry before attaching figures to the bulletin board. This shredded yarn will give a 3-D effect.

Suggested Color Scheme

Background: royal blue bulletin board paper.

Border and letters: white construction paper with lettering in permanent black or royal blue marker. (This is an excellent opportunity to use calligraphy.)

Dove: white tagboard covered with white shredded yarn.

Flames: red construction paper covered with red, orange, and gold shredded yarn.

Heart: red construction paper covered with red shredded yarn.

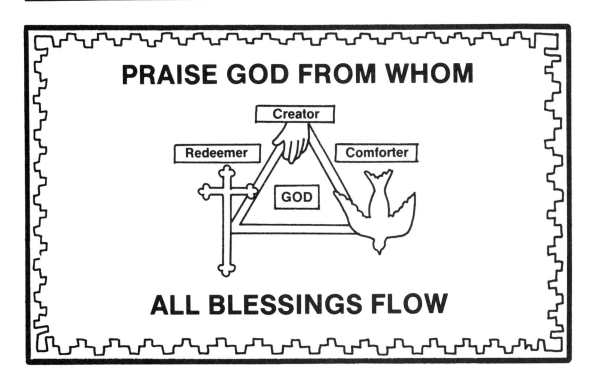

Praise God

The Trinity is indeed to be praised! This bulletin board is especially effective during the Trinity season but is appropriate at any time of the year. The triangle is used as a universal symbol for the concept of three persons—One God. This concept is somewhat broadened by using names "Creator, Redeemer, and Comforter" instead of the more familiar "Father, Son, and Holy Spirit." One symbol is shown to represent each of the members of the Trinity, thus reminding the viewer of the unique work of each person in the Trinity.

Suggested Color Scheme

Background: royal blue bulletin board paper.

Border and letters: white construction paper.

Triangle: white construction paper cut in strips 1¼″ wide and of an appropriate length to form a triangle suitable for the size of the bulletin board to be used.

Dove: white construction paper (see pattern on page 88).

Hand: white construction paper outlined in permanent black marker and colored with flesh-color crayons.

Cross: gold foil.

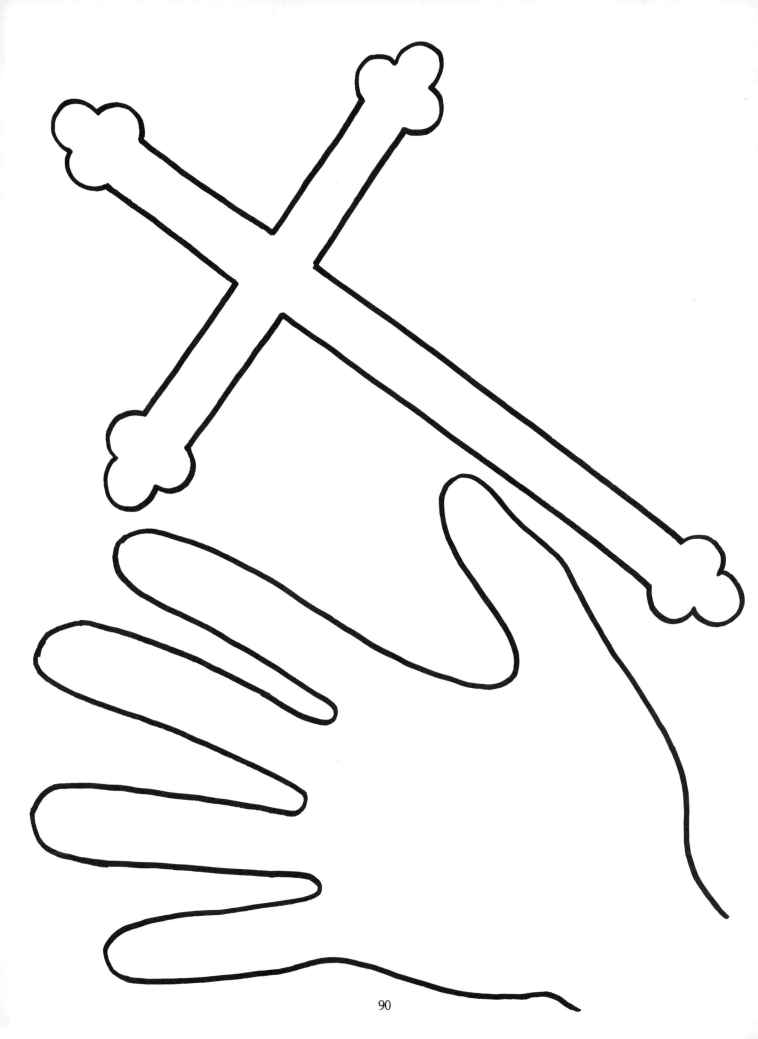

90

God Gives Us New Beginnings

The cross is the focal point of this graduation theme, just as it should be our focal point in life. This theme gives all glory and honor to God for His gifts to the graduate rather than on the graduate himself. The usual graduation symbols—the mortarboard and the diploma—are given a new meaning when combined with the rose, a symbol of God's creation; the cross, a symbol of Christ's work of salvation; and the dove and flame, symbols of the Holy Spirit's work in our lives.

Suggested Color Scheme

Background: white bulletin board paper.

Border and letters: royal blue construction paper.

Mortarboard and Bible: pale blue (or whatever the colors of a particular graduating class for which the bulletin board is used).

Flame: white construction paper colored red, orange, and gold using permanent markers (see pattern on page 87).

Dove: white construction paper (see pattern on page 88).

Cross: gold foil (see pattern on page 90).

Diploma: off-white parchment paper rolled and tied with narrow white ribbon or white construction paper pattern tied with ribbon (see pattern on page 92).

Rose: white construction paper colored red and green with permanent markers.

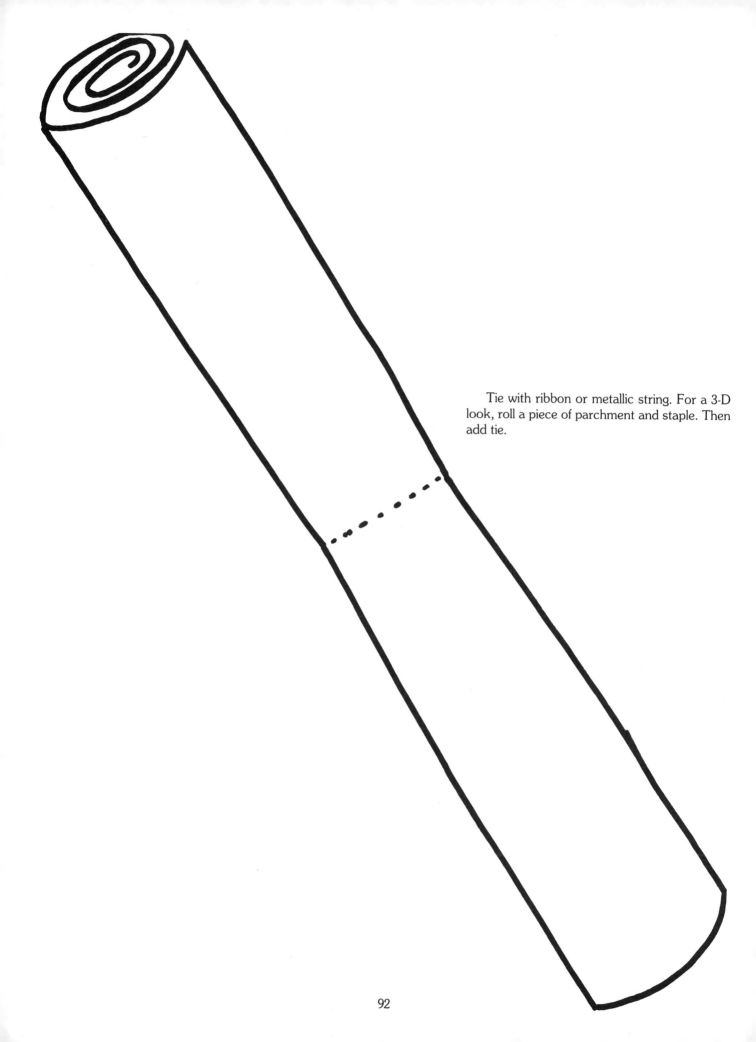

Tie with ribbon or metallic string. For a 3-D look, roll a piece of parchment and staple. Then add tie.

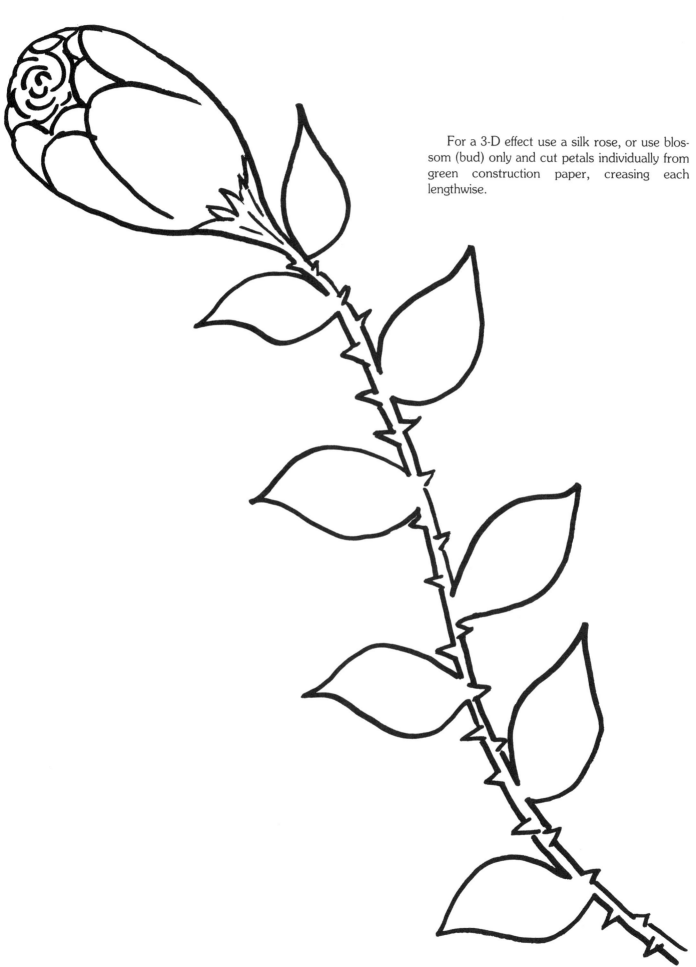

For a 3-D effect use a silk rose, or use blossom (bud) only and cut petals individually from green construction paper, creasing each lengthwise.

HOLY
BIBLE

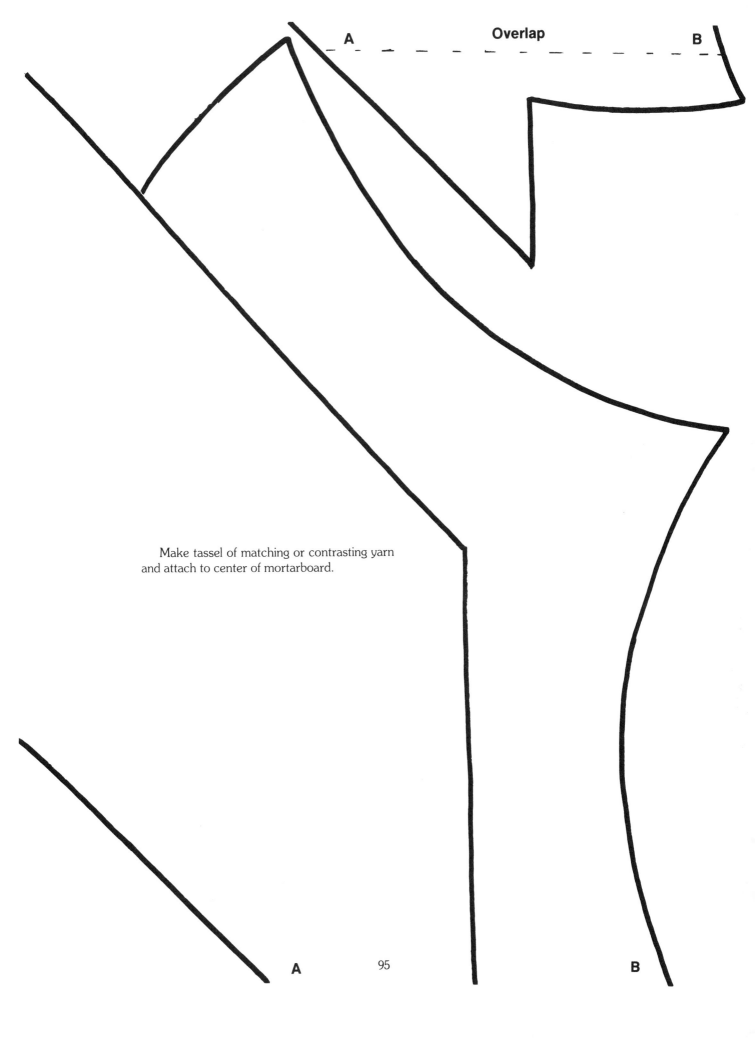

A   **Overlap**   **B**

Make tassel of matching or contrasting yarn
and attach to center of mortarboard.

A   95   **B**

June

Be Thou Our Guide

The Word of the Lord is at the heart this graduation theme. Graduation is portrayed as a beginning of a life for which God's guidance is both requested and accepted.

If bulletin board space is adequate, it would be desirable to include Ps. 25:4-5. These verses would be especially effective in calligraphy.

The mortarboard and diploma symbolize commencement of a new phase of life, while the olive branches symbolize God's promise of a new life with Him.

Suggested Color Scheme

Background: white bulletin board paper.

Border and letters: royal blue construction paper (or the colors of the particular graduating class).

Mortarboard and diploma: white construction paper outlined with class color; ribbon around diploma and tassel on mortar board may also be done in class colors. (See patterns on pages 92 and 95.)

Open Bible: see pattern on page 57.

Cross bookmark: small cross may be cut from gold foil or an inexpensive jewelry cross may be used.

Olive branch: green construction paper. (See pattern on page 82.)

These pages have illustrated many ideas for Christian bulletin boards. However, the possibilities are nearly endless. Almost every Scripture verse can be illustrated to present a meaningful message.

Many materials can be used effectively. Patterns for symbols, letters, and borders are everywhere. Best of all, bulletin boards dedicated to the glory of God carry with them a promise:

"So shall My word be that goeth forth out of My mouth: it shall not return unto Me void, but it shall accomplish that which I please, and it shall prosper in the thing whereto I sent it" (Is. 55:11).